Above
and Below

by Christopher Stitt

illustrated by

Chris Norris

A Harcourt Achieve Imprint

www.Steck-Vaughn.com
1-800-531-5015

Above and Below

Steck-Vaughn Crossroads
Originally published as Laser Beams © 2001

Blake Publishing Pty Ltd, 108 Main Road,
Clayton South VIC 3168, Australia

Exclusive United States Distribution: Harcourt Achieve Inc.
Harcourt Achieve Inc.
10801 N. Mopac Exp., Bldg. 3
Austin, Texas 78759
www.HarcourtAchieve.com

ISBN-13: 978-1-4189-4524-4
ISBN-10:   1-4189-4524-2

Printed in China

1 2 3 4 5 6 7 8 788 14 13 12 11 10 09 08 07

Contents

Chapter 1

A Better Place Than This

Jakob sits staring at the large boulder that separates his world from the world above. "If only I could move it and see what the Above World is like," he says.

"You shouldn't speak like that," scolds Tibalt. "If the guards hear you—"

Jakob stands. "I'm not scared of Zelig's guards. Gerlat has told me stories of the Above World."

Tibalt laughs. "Gerlat is old and his mind is failing. Anyway, our people came underground months before he was born. How could he know about the Above World?"

Jakob and Tibalt are best friends, but sometimes Tibalt makes Jakob angry. Why can't Tibalt dream? Why can't he imagine a place better than the cold, dark world they live in?

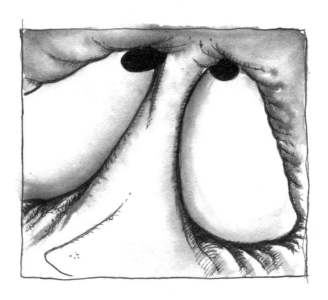

Jakob is a dreamer. He's seen many of his friends battle the illnesses brought on by the damp conditions that surround them, and he knows they aren't supposed to live like this. Jakob believes what Gerlat has told him about a better place that lies above.

"We should get to school," suggests Tibalt.

Jakob looks up at the boulder. "I just want to see if it's true, that's all. A tiny peek."

"There's nothing to see. The Above World was destroyed in the Great Destruction and is unfit for human life now," says Tibalt.

Jakob's eyes gleam. "What if the Destruction never happened?"

"Of course it did," Tibalt says.

"You don't know that for sure. Gerlat said it didn't." Jakob picks up his lantern filled with fireflies. "The Above World may be just as our ancestors left it."

Tibalt follows him back down the dark passageways. "We've been taught all about the Great Destruction in our lessons. If the Destruction never happened, why would we be down here?"

Jakob and Tibalt arrive in the school chamber as Zelig, the leader of the Underground, is about to begin the lesson. Zelig's family has always led the Underground. Zelig took over the leadership when both his parents died from eating poisonous mushrooms. He has been the leader for as long as Jakob can remember.

"We will continue our lesson on the Great Destruction that destroyed the Above World seventy years ago," begins Zelig. "Who can tell me what caused the Great Destruction?"

Tibalt raises his hand high. "Lack of water, sir. They used too much water."

"That's right, but how did the lack of water cause the Destruction?"

Tibalt's sister raises her hand. "Plants didn't have enough water to grow, so the people and animals didn't have enough food."

"Who predicted the Destruction?"

"Ingel, the village healer," says Tibalt.

Zelig walks over to Tibalt and asks, "What did he predict would happen?"

"The land would become a desert, and rain would not fall," Tibalt replies.

"Correct!" Zelig's eyes blaze in the lamplight and his pale skin shines. "Our people gathered provisions and came below before the Destruction could destroy us. We found the underground spring and built a safe world below the ground."

Jakob raises his hand.

Zelig peers down at Jakob and asks, "You have a question?"

14

"What if there was no Destruction?" asks Jakob.

"Who fills your head with such nonsense?" Zelig booms.

"Gerlat told me," replies Jakob.

Zelig marches over to Jakob. "Gerlat is a fool who has filled your head with lies. You must never speak to him again."

Jakob stands and retorts, "Maybe you're the fool. What if Gerlat is right? Shouldn't we find out?"

What do you think of Jakob's response to Zelig?

"How dare you defy me!" Zelig glares at Jakob.

Jakob knows it isn't wise to argue with Zelig, so he stands up and dashes from the school chamber.

Chapter 2

Talking to Gerlat

Gerlat's parents came underground five months before Gerlat was born. His grandfather had stayed in the Above World.

After his father's death, Gerlat had found an old letter from his grandfather explaining why his grandfather had not gone underground. It described the beauty of the Above World and his grandfather's distrust of Ingel, the village healer.

After Jakob leaves the school chamber, he finds Gerlat sitting in the fungi gardens, a damp and musty chamber where various mushrooms are grown for food. It is one of the places where Gerlat goes to think.

"I'm glad I found you," puffs Jakob. "I'm ready to go up to the surface. I can't stay here anymore. I want to show them all the truth."

Gerlat takes Jakob's hand. "Sit."

Jakob sits in front of the old man and says, "Yes, Gerlat?"

Gerlat holds his finger to his lip and glances over his shoulders. "You must whisper. You never know who's around. What happened?"

"Zelig keeps teaching about the Great Destruction. He won't listen to what I have to say," Jakob replies.

"Be careful of Zelig. Don't get on his bad side," Gerlat warns.

"I think it's too late."

Gerlat looks deeply into Jakob's big, blue eyes and says, "I found all the old records today."

"How?" Jakob replies excitedly, leaning closer. "I thought they were destroyed!"

Gerlat pulls out some tattered, brown pages from under his cloak. "Zelig has had them all along. There is no record of Ingel ever coming underground. The healer stayed on the surface. My grandfather was right not to trust Ingel."

"I must go," says Gerlat, standing and looking around the gardens. "Dark corners are perfect places for spies to hide. I'll speak with you soon when it is less dangerous. Zelig will be looking for you."

"But Gerlat—"

Is Jakob right to trust Gerlat? Explain.

Gerlat vanishes into the darkness. As Jakob
sits in the chamber, listening to the drip,
drip, drip of water from the stalactites,
he is in no hurry to return to his home
chamber. Zelig is sure to have spoken to
his parents.

Chapter 3

Standing Up
for Your Beliefs

Jakob walks slowly home. He isn't worried about being late for supper. He's already done far worse that day—he's questioned their leader.

From the tunnel, Jakob sees lamplight blazing through the window of his home chamber and smells supper cooking on the fire. He opens the door.

"Where have you been?" asks Jakob's father, Amory.

"I'm sorry. I lost track of time," Jakob replies quickly.

Della, Jakob's mother, pours mushroom stew into three bowls and says, "Supper will be ruined if we don't eat it now."

No one says much during supper. Jakob finishes his stew as quickly as possible and then picks up his empty bowl and says, "May I be excused?"

Amory looks at his son. "Jakob, Zelig came here to speak to us about your behavior at school. Why did you question him?"

"I don't believe him. Why does everyone always think he is right? Why is it wrong to question him?" replies Jakob.

"Our history is written," Della says sternly.

"Written by Zelig's father," snaps Jakob.

"Zelig doesn't want you to see Gerlat any more," says Amory.

Jakob looks around his dark, damp home chamber and dreams of the world Gerlat has told him about—dry and warm, with fresh air to breathe. "I will keep seeing Gerlat," Jakob insists. "Why does everyone think he's crazy? What if he's right? We live in this cold, dark hole when we could live in the light and beauty of the Above World, where we belong."

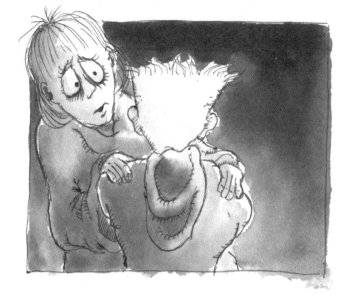

Della hugs her son and says, "Even if Gerlat is right, you can't upset Zelig. As our leader, he can make our lives very difficult."

Jakob wishes he could promise his mother that he won't upset Zelig, but something greater is at stake. As he walks to the front door, he says "I'll prove it to you all."

What does Jakob mean when he decides "something greater is at stake"?

Jakob makes his way through the darkened tunnels to Gerlat's home chamber, but no light shines in the window. Jakob's heart pounds as he knocks on the door. When no one answers, he slowly turns the knob. The door is unlocked, and Gerlat is nowhere to be seen. Papers are scattered over the floor as though someone has been looking for something.

Jakob knows Gerlat would not leave it this way. Who has done this? Where is Gerlat?

Jakob feels a hand touch his shoulder and jumps with fright. He turns, expecting to see Zelig or one of Zelig's guards, but is surprised to see Tibalt instead. "What are you doing here?" asks Jakob.

"Looking for you. You weren't at home so I thought you might be here," Tibalt whispers, pulling Jakob into the shadows. "I saw Zelig and his guards here earlier, going through Gerlat's things."

"Did they hurt Gerlat?" asks Jakob.

"Gerlat wasn't here," says Tibalt.

"They must be after the old records Gerlat found. We need to get out of here," says Jakob as he heads out the door.

"What? Where are we going?" asks Tibalt.

"The crystal gardens, one of the places Gerlat goes to be alone. He might be there." Jakob turns to Tibalt. "Are you coming?"

Chapter 4

Crystal Gardens

Jakob leads Tibalt through the tunnels, passing guards all along the way. This peaceful underground city has little need for guards, but they add to Zelig's power.

Jakob and Tibalt arrive at the crystal
gardens, a huge chamber filled with
strange, pale, beautiful limestone
formations that glitter in the light from the
firefly lanterns. Long, thin stalactites hang
from the ceiling and chunky stalagmites
rise up from the floor.

"Why would you want to leave this?"
Tibalt says, looking around in awe. This is
his favorite place.

"Gerlat has read descriptions of the surface that are much more beautiful than this," answers Jakob.

Jakob walks over to a large stalagmite and looks behind it. "Glad I found you," he says to Gerlat, who is hiding there.

Startled, Gerlat turns around. He hadn't heard the boys. "I'm glad you're on my side. You know all my hide-outs." Gerlat is surprised to see Tibalt and asks, "What brings you here as well?"

"I listened to what Jakob said today about the Above World. He believes you and was prepared to stand up to Zelig. I want to know if it's true," says Tibalt.

Footsteps echo along the tunnel leading to the gardens. Jakob and Tibalt quickly hide behind the stalagmite with Gerlat as two guards enter.

They can hear the guards talking as the guards search for Gerlat. Jakob holds his breath in fear. If the guards catch them, they will be brought before Zelig and lose any chance of ever going to the surface. It is tonight or never. As the guards turn and leave, Jakob feels hope.

Jakob turns to Gerlat. "I have to go to the surface tonight. If I don't go now, Zelig will try to stop me," he whispers.

"I don't know. I don't want to put you in danger. We don't really know what the surface is like," says a worried Gerlat.

"I'll go with him," says Tibalt. "We can look after each other."

Jakob turns to his friend. "Are you sure?"

Tibalt nods.

Chapter 5

Breaking Through

Gerlat leads the boys to his tunnel. "I've been secretly digging this tunnel for years. I haven't broken through to the surface yet, but I am sure that I'm close," says Gerlat.

Jakob and Tibalt each take a spade and begin digging. Although both of them dig for several hours, they do not break though. It is taking longer than any of them had expected.

"I was sure I was close," Gerlat says, looking at his plans. "Could I have been wrong?"

With all his strength, Jakob shoves his
spade into the soft earth above. The boys
shield their eyes as the dirt falls around
them. A small stream of light pierces the
darkness of the tunnel.

Gerlat races to the hole, squinting his eyes
in the light. "Smells all right," he says.
"I think we've made it!"

Jakob and Tibalt want to cheer, but
instead they dig as quickly as they can.
As Jakob and Tibalt continue enlarging
the hole, light unlike anything they've ever
experienced spills down the walls of the
tunnel. Fireflies and glow-worms don't light
things up like this.

"It's big enough now," says Jakob.
"This is it!"

As Tibalt starts to help Jakob up toward the light, they hear movement behind them. "Stop!" commands Zelig from the dark tunnel. "You cannot go to the surface." He and four guards move into the light.

Gerlat turns to Zelig. "You can't stop them now."

"I am leader of The Underground, so I can do as I please. You all will rot in a cell for this treason," shrieks Zelig.

Jakob isn't going to let Zelig ruin this. They've come so far. He looks at Gerlat, who nods and turns to face the guards.

Tibalt pushes Jakob through the hole.

"Stop!" yells Zelig. "Stop!"

Tibalt throws his spade at the guards and
grasps Jakob's hands. He, too, vanishes
into the light.

"Hurry, boys. Prove me right!" calls Gerlat.

Two of the guards run forward, grab
Gerlat, and force his arms behind his back.

Chapter 6

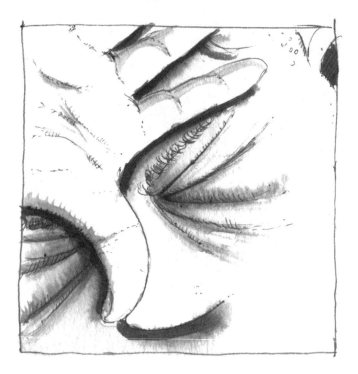

The Above World

Jakob struggles to keep his eyes open in light so much brighter than anything he's seen before. He shields his eyes with his hand and tries to scan the strange, new world stretching around him.

Tibalt squints. "It's so bright—so much brighter than glow-worms."

Jakob looks back at the hole and says, "I don't see Zelig or the guards. Do you think he'll send someone to capture us?"

"I hope not," answers Tibalt.

As their eyes adjust to the light, the boys
look around, stunned by the space,
shapes, and colors of the Above World.
Jakob crouches down to the ground. "This
green stuff feels really nice," he says,
stroking the grass. "I wonder if you can
eat it."

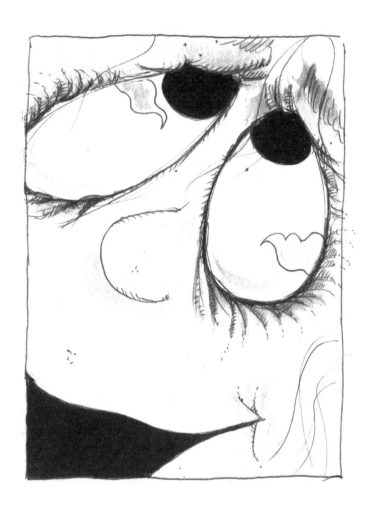

"Wow! Look up there! That must be the sky my grandmother told me about. It's amazing how big it is!" Tibalt stares upward with his mouth open.

The boys walk across the grass to the
edge of a hill looking down at a small
village.

"Look at those funny homes," Tibalt says,
pointing. "I wonder what it's like to live in
one of those."

"What's wrong with my cottage?" says a
voice behind them.

They turn to see a girl in a brightly colored dress standing with her hands on her hips.

"Do you know about the Great Destruction?" asks Jakob.

The girl looks at Jakob strangely and says, "Great Destruction? Huh? What are you talking about?"

When Jakob tells the girl about the Great Destruction and how they live under the ground, she says, "That explains why you look as though you've been locked away for years. You could use some sunshine and fresh air."

As Jakob continues his story about the Great Destruction that Ingel had predicted, the girl laughs and tells them nothing like that ever happened.

"What about the water?" asks Tibalt. "Did it run out?"

The girl laughs again. "No. We have plenty of water."

"This is not a joke," says Tibalt as calmly as he can.

The girl stops laughing because she can see by the look on Tibalt's face that they are telling the truth. "You had better come to my village," she says. "By the way, my name is Felda."

People stare at Jakob and Tibalt and crowd around them as they walk through the village. Felda stops outside a large cottage.

A tall man comes out of the cottage and asks, "Who have you got with you, Felda?"

"I found them on the hill. They come from underground."

Chapter 7

Beyond the Boulder

Jakob and Tibalt sit down with the villagers and Felda's father, Baldric, the village chief. They eat food with the most amazing flavors—sweet, juicy fruit, and bread mixed with herbs, all washed down with a cool drink of milk.

"Ingel predicted the Great Destruction," begins Jakob.

"Ingel!" gasps one of the villagers. "Just as my father said."

Jakob turns to the old man who has spoken. "You know Ingel?"

"I know of him." The old man leans closer to Jakob. "My father knew him. Ingel told my father how he tricked a whole village into going underground."

"Why? How did Ingel do this?" Baldric scoffs, eyebrows raised.

"Just as Jakob said. Ingel wanted to keep the water for himself and his followers. He never went underground," replies the old man.

"But we have plenty of water," says Felda, her mouth full of bread.

"My grandfather told about a time of great drought," remembers Baldric. "But he said heavy rains fell the following year, and we've had plenty of water ever since."

Jakob stands. "Zelig lied to us, and he may hurt Gerlat for defying him. Please help us save our people. Why should they live in those dark tunnels when they can live here?"

"We'll help you. Show us where you live," says Baldric.

Jakob and Tibalt lead the villagers to the
hill where they had emerged into the
Above World, but they cannot find the
hole. "I'm sure it was here," says Jakob.

"Zelig must have filled the hole," Tibalt
says, sighing.

"I'm certain Gerlat is being punished,
even as we speak. We have to save him,"
pleads Jakob.

"There must be another way," suggests Baldric.

Jakob thinks hard and then exclaims, "The boulder! At the end of a tunnel in the Below World is a large boulder that Gerlat says separates the two worlds. Have you seen a large boulder in the ground near here?"

"I've seen a big boulder in the other side of the hill," says Felda. She shows everyone where the large boulder lies.

"This must be it," Jakob says hopefully.

"Let's move it," says Baldric as he places his hands on the boulder. "If we all work together, I think we can move it."

Jakob, Tibalt, and all the villagers move in against the boulder, pushing with all their might as sweat drips down their faces.

Finally, the boulder begins to move. Slowly it rocks and then suddenly it rolls out of the way, revealing a dimly lit tunnel.

"This is it!" shouts Jakob.

"You need to lead us, Jakob," says Baldric.

Jakob nods, feeling as if his stomach is
tied in knots. Hoping they will find Gerlat
safe, he takes a lantern from the wall of
the tunnel to light their way.

Chapter 8

A New Life

As the villagers follow Jakob and Tibalt through the tunnels, Tibalt says, "Something is wrong."

Jakob holds up the lantern and says, "Where is everyone? The tunnels are too quiet."

As they reach the main chamber, they see a large crowd gathered inside. Zelig stands on a platform in front of Gerlat, who is held tightly by two guards.

"What should we do now?" whispers Baldric.

"Wait a bit. I want to hear what Zelig has to say," says Jakob.

"This man has caused some of our people to commit treason," Zelig says, pointing to Gerlat. "He must be punished for filling our children's heads with false stories denying the Destruction. He must be stopped."

"Zelig lies to you," shouts Gerlat. "There was no—" One of the guards hits Gerlat to silence him.

"Quiet, old man," spits Zelig. "Gerlat allowed two boys to enter the Above World. Sadly, Jakob and Tibalt are gone forever."

Jakob hears the crowd gasp and sees his
parents' worried faces. As Jakob's mother
bursts into tears, Jakob's father holds her
tightly. "Maybe Gerlat speaks the truth.
We must see for ourselves. We must go to
the surface and find the boys," he cries.

"Never!" shouts Zelig. "I'm shocked at you,
Amory. You will be imprisoned with Gerlat.
I won't allow you to endanger others."

Jakob has heard enough and can wait no
longer. He climbs up onto a large rock and
shouts, "It's over, Zelig. Gerlat speaks the
truth. There was no Great Destruction.
We were all tricked."

The crowd gasps in shock to see Jakob and
Tibalt. Della and Amory run to their son.

Zelig suddenly looks afraid and backs
away, shouting, "This is a trick. You must
not believe them!"

"No trick," shouts Jakob as his new friends
walk into the chamber.

Baldric joins Jakob on the rock. "Jakob speaks the truth. We live on the surface, but have experienced no Destruction. Ingel tricked your people so he could keep the water for himself."

"How did you survive without any water?" asks Amory.

"Heavy rains fell soon after your people went underground. We use our water wisely and have had no water shortages. We invite you to join us above ground," says Baldric kindly.

"Zelig has known all this," announces Gerlat. "He likes the power he holds, and he fears he would lose it in the Above World."

As Zelig tries to escape, his own guards grab him.

Slowly, the people of the Underground smile as they think of leaving their cold, dark homes to begin a new life in the Above World.

Glossary

ancestors (*noun*) family members who lived many years ago

awe (*noun*) respect mixed with wonder

chamber (*noun*) a room

defy (*verb*) challenge; resist; question

pierces (*verb*) forces through or makes a way into

predicted (*verb*) told something that would happen in the future

revealing (*verb*) uncovering; showing

shield (*verb*) protect with a cover; shelter

squinting (*verb*) partly closing the eyes

stalactites (*noun*) pieces of stone shaped like icicles that hang from the ceiling of a cave

stalagmites (*noun*) pieces of stone shaped like icicles that form on the floor of a cave

treason (*noun*) the act of being unfaithful to one's own country

Idioms

at stake (*page 29*) depending on it; at risk

A Deeper Look

ancestors
• Ancestors are family members who came before our grandparents. The English word *ancestor* comes from some Latin words that mean "to go before."

predict
• Synonyms: foretell, forecast, guess
• Does a weather reporter predict yesterday's weather or tomorrow's weather?

Take It Further
Many people enjoy learning about their ancestors. Do you know where your ancestors lived, what languages they spoke, or what kinds of food they ate?

Talk Back!

Hello, everyone. This is Jakob talking to you from the awesome Above World. I've had a chance to think about our adventure, and I'd like to know what you think, too.

• I feel it's important to stand up for what you believe, even when it's hard to do. What risks did I take to find out whether Zelig was telling us the truth? How could I have found out in a safer way?

• What have you done to find out whether a person was telling the truth or acting fairly?

Now that we've talked, tell me more about what you think.

 Get together with a friend to talk about and write answers to these questions.

1. What kinds of problems can happen when leaders have too much power? How do people set up governments to keep those kinds of problems from happening?

2. What kinds of freedoms and rights are important to protect so people won't be afraid of their government? Together, make a poster listing the five rights you feel are most important for citizens of a society.